CH00869305

Beauty for Ashes

Debrecia Echols

Forward

I dedicate this book to my Lord and Savior Jesus Christ. Without him I am nothing!

~Debrecia

Table of Contents

- The Narcissist
- Broken
- Python Spirit
- Singleness
- Healing
- Counterfeit
- Ashes Burned

The Narcissist

Here I go again! You would think I would have got it right by learning how
to trust God on every decision I made in my life. I never even knew such
things existed as that personality behavior. To get the full concept of what I
dealt with, you will need the definition of what narcissist behavior is.
Webster defines it as: A personality disorder characterized especially by an
exaggerated sense of self-importance, persistent need for admiration, lack
of empathy for others, excessive pride in achievements, and snobbish,
disdainful, or patronizing attitudes. If I may add in my own word a self-
centered, egotist, and show-off. Yep that's who I had married and,
he kept it so hidden. On top of what the dictionary does not define: He
was always right and, I guess to him I was the incompetent one? It often
left me angry and, with the feeling of having to defend myself, often having
negative self-images about myself. Everything was everyone else's fault
and, he could never apologize when wrong. I'd often find myself
apologizing even when things were not even my fault. He started out as
alluring and attractive., especially during the initial stages of the
relationship. I didn't know that was to win me over. Yes, that charming and

romantic came with a catch. Like a master salesperson, he used seduction and flattery to sweep me off my feet but, wanted to extract from me to fulfill the emptiness due to his inability to create true intimacy. I was told from a prophet ten years later, that the relationship was to keep me from my God-given purpose and assignment. I should have went to college to be a relationship therapist. You name it, it happened. I have been through every unimaginable thing you could possibly think of. I only existed to serve his needs. I was expected to be "on call" and satisfy his sexual desires and, at his pleasure. I was required to engage in sexual acts that he only enjoyed, and he demanded that I limit any other activity I had going on. Rather than being my own individual with my own thoughts, feelings, and priorities, he expected me to exist for his own wishes. My own needs were often dismissed and ignored. You are probably thinking why didn't I just leave right? I often ask myself the same question. There were a lot of spiritual forces behind the relationship that I could not see. I said maybe if my discernment was on point, I would not have missed it, just maybe right? It's why we have to be so in tune to God, even though we are living in a practical world, in this physical body, we are still a spirit being. We do not wrestle against flesh and blood and, we know that that devil he is real. I've heard a statement before: "Some people try to be tall by cutting off the heads of others". I'm not sure who quoted that but, yes his disguised insecurities and inadequacy was to try and put me down to boost his own acceptance. I've always been secure in who I was but, being married to that personality had me question my own abilities as a woman of God. The thoughts of was I good enough and, am I accepted? There were thoughts of ridicule, blame, shame, and all while being run by manipulation to make me feel that I was inferior. This was a psychological war and, it was trying to take me out at any cost necessary. He was able to gain a greater degree of dominance, and manipulation. The more I would say no or didn't give him what he wanted, the more he was angry and threw tantrums. There was always some negative judgement and, some type of personal attack against me. The more I prayed seem like the more he got worse. I was often given the cold shoulder, or silent treatment as a way of punishment. I was withheld love and affection often being told that I was ungrateful. How could I be ungrateful when the majority of the responsibility was on me to do? He would often play the victim and, non of his responses would be those of a responsible matured, responsible adult. He would often act like a child and a bully, with hopes that his drama would hook me back in, so that I would once again "belong" to him. I encourage you if you are in that kind of relationship, run for your life and never look back. In the midst of the chaos, the jealousy when I tried to succeed, I came to realize he just didn't want to see me happy. What he showed me was truly who he was. No matter the prophecies he received about his calling and, almost literally everywhere he went, nothing had changed. He hardened his heart towards God, therefore forcing me to make the choice to walk away after 10 years. I chose God! There was not anything that could change my mind. After all the suffering that I endured, enough was enough! No man would have the power any longer to belittle my faith and my God. I would never let anyone else in that close anymore. Well, that's what I thought.

Broken

I was broken and there was no other way to put it. I thought about what the word says. The Lord being close to the brokenhearted, he saved me because, I was crushed in my spirit. It was so difficult to recognize this because, I was in it for so long. This time I didn't have to call my parents in the middle of the night to get me because he stole my car. This time it wasn't my red eye from being hit, or being hit in the face with a laundry basket for trying to leave. This time it wasn't the spit to my face, or the broken right index finger from him snatching my keys away. This time it wasn't the chokes, the pushes, the name calling, the throwing juice in my new hairstyle. This time it wasn't the yelling, cursing, throwing chairs, the B word, him talking about my family was better than his. This time it wasn't the bladder infections, my body growing tumors from stress, him wishing death on me because, I mentioned his ways were just pure evil. This time it wasn't calling the police after he hit me and I pushed him back only to try and get me in trouble. This time it wasn't the constant badgering of him threatening to take my car every other week because his name was on the registration too. No, something had shifted inside of me, and that made me stone cold. I was broken, no other words to say but that. I had no clue how God was going to get me out of this. Once I came to the realization, that he was who he was no matter how much he said sorry, I knew it was a done deal.

I literally felt as if I was bleeding on the inside. This was someone who I'd planned on spending the rest of my life with. I could remember the "your family doesn't care about you", or "you'll be lost without me" comments. I'd stopped preparing for him to change. But, at sudden moments he would start doing the things that he felt I was complaining about. The main one for me was going to church and, having a personal relationship with Jesus. The brokenness that I felt was brutal and painful. He was too charming, engaging, and charismatic, which made it even more difficult to leave in the first place. I never knew who I was waking up to everyday. One minute I felt like I was everything he had ever wanted, and the next I was left wondering what on Earth went wrong. He played that role while getting something from me, the source. It was draining me both mentally and physically, to the point where I began to grow tumors inside of my womb. The enemy was killing me slowly inside, and I didn't even recognize it. I lived with it first hand for ten years. I often experienced what's called gas lighting being married to him. Webster defines it as: feeling the need to apologize for constantly being at fault, even if the argument or conflict is started by your partner. It was designed to make me lack trust in my own senses, memories, and actions. Any type of recollections that I reminded him of were often dismissed as not even occurring. He would have what

I would to call selective memories. It was literally impossible to recognize and, therefore would cause me to have emotional distress. It's how the enemy used him to try and trap me. This was a psychological battle only God could break me free of.

This battle had me broken into pieces. I had never been one to be put down by anyone or anything. When I failed to respond to his "superior" it triggered rage and there was definitely a retribution I had to pay. I guess he thought he was unique, and I was supposed to give him in his mind, the desire he deserved. There was some kind of magical thinking to have me feel, that all the good things in my life came from him. Anything that was negative happened to be distorted or the fault of someone else, typically me the partner. I was the blame for not living up to his expectations of the perfect wife, the image he created. Any minor upset would blow up, and he would leave with bags in hands only to ostracize me, and the turn the phone off. It was a trick to have me feel abandonment and having the fear of being left. I was to beg and plead like a child whose mother had disappeared out of her sight while shopping. I would therefore do whatever he wanted. This was abuse! It was manipulative, and the very definition of emotional abuse. I didn't deserve this. There was no right to leave because I asked for some reciprocity in the marriage. It was very, very traumatic, and it will take a toll on your mental and physical well-being. I almost died, and suffered serious physical injuries from the abuse. I left someone who had me feeling repeatedly abandoned and ostracized. It can kill you, and if you have any doubts ask me.

Python Spirit

If you have every read my book Answer the Call, then you will know that God deals with me in dreams and visions. I have also seen and experience things in the spirit realm. That is a gift that God has given me from the age of 8 years old. I will never forget this day that I saw the python. When you think of python, you think of a snake. God allowed me to see the spirit of this python snake wrapped around my ex-husband. As I was asleep in the bed I was suddenly awakened in my spirit. I could feel something in the room. As God opened my sprit to see, I could see my ex-husband physically laying in the bed but, his spirit in the form of a man was standing up. I could then see this big black snake wrapped around him, with the head and mouth of the snake speaking in his ear. I then realized that I was in my spirit and what God was showing me. I gasped, because this snake was huge and it was scary. I immediately woke up, looked over at him and got out of the bed. I went into my prayer room to pray. At the time, I knew it was a snake/spirit but I didn't know what kind of spirit that it was. I needed to know it's purpose, what it was there for, and how to get him delivered from it. Little did I know that snake was sent for me. I then later that day called my spiritual mom, and friend to pray and to find out what I was dealing with. We then came to the conclusion the snake I saw wrapped around him, squeezing the life out of him, was a spirit of the Python.

I never understood why every time I would pray it seemed like my prayers were hitting a wall. It seemed like nothing was effective. Every time I had to speak, minister, pray, or even prepare for church he would frustrate me so bad to the point we would be in a yelling match before service. I would literally go into the office in the other room to pray and seek God's face. Times I would have to lead prayer before service, any kind of distraction would try and throw me off so I could not be effective in prayer. I then began to study what I saw, how to handle it, and how to speak directly to it once it began to strike. It literally squeezed the joy out of me, my worship, and my prayers. It wanted to pressure me to keep quiet when God wanted me to speak up. There were times it would try to insult my God, and it was that spirit that stole my peace. In the spirit realm, Satan worked the same way through my ex-husband. He slowly used my ex to slither into my life, thus attempting to choke out my joy, peace, courage, and success; thus piling on the pressure until I felt defeated. With Jesus, I had the victory. Another time I could remember him shaving as I walked pass the bathroom door. I was on my way to church and when I looked, I saw his eyes pupils looked like that of a snake. As I stopped in my tracks, I immediately jumped back against the wall. I begin to stare a little closer in the spirit and I could see it so clearly. My God in Heaven I thought at that very moment. Surely as it noticed I saw it, my ex-husband began to start an argument. I begin to rebuke that spirit, and all kinds of scriptures begin to flow out of my mouth. As, I looked and battled this spirit one on one, I began to crush his head by praying aggressive and violent. I could not afford to be lady like, but by fervent prayers and fasting was the way I defeated it coming against me. I also had to ask God to forgive me from allowing in anything that may have opened the door for it to enter. Once it was called out, it was then revealed that my ex-husband mom's family was into witchcraft, and it connected to me physically by sex with him. It was the reason my womb was having so many problems both physically and spiritually. I eventually had to have surgery from the four tumors that grew as large as a newborn baby's head. Once the doctors went in, I was told afterwards that I would not be able to have any more kids. There was no way possible because, others organs were damaged. I was devastated but knew, that because of my prolonging the situation by staying in that marriage, I eventually would have died a slow spiritual and maybe physical death. I had all kinds of emotions and regrets now that I couldn't have any more kids. There was definitely one emotion, and that was anger. Most of that anger was towards myself for staying in the situation for as long as I did. I began to blame myself and have a self-pity party. God quickly reminded me that there was nothing to hard, that I could not handle. I was much stronger now than I ever knew before. There was a purpose behind the reason and a purpose for this happening in my life. How can you tell anyone anything if you've never gone through? If only life were that simple. This too would be part of my

Singleness

Where do I go from here? That is the question I asked myself. I knew that I had to escape. How do you give ten years of your life and start over? I had really grown comfortable but, God allowed the circumstances to push me out. There was no other way to put it but to get out. This was one of the toughest decisions I ever had to make in life, I thought. From all the prophecies that God would use me in a mighty way, to his calling you would think it would be all good. The longer I stayed the worse it became. I knew that the dream I had it was time to go. I gave him an ultimatum that he either totally choose God or lose me. He needed to get delivered of that spirit but he chose to keep it. It got to the point that I asked God to begin to reveal things to him in the spirit realm. One early morning after 4 am he yelled and jumped out of bed. God allowed him to see that same snake spirit coiled and wrapped around his leg. I will never forget that morning he woke me up screaming from fear. I quietly mentioned "your eyes are open now". I got out of bed and went into the office/room to pray. God was trying to get his attention but, he still wasn't listening. There was nothing else that God needed to show me. It was time to go. I filed for divorce that October and was gone with only my car and my clothes. I walked away from everything. I didn't want anything from the house that would remind me of being with him. It wasn't easy to do but, it was necessary. Fear tried to grip me that I wouldn't be able to go on in life without him. He had tried to install in my brain that I wouldn't make it. From being told that my family didn't love me, and that he was the only one that was there for me it was kind of scary. I had thoughts of going back to that but, God said I would surely die if I did. I almost lost my life due to stress and those tumors. I researched the spiritual root cause of what I had been previously diagnosed with. For every physical ailment there is a spiritual root cause to that sickness or disease. For fibroids it was a woman having here feminity/ego hurt from a man or male. I was like wow God. So many times I can remember of just keeping my feelings suppressed, kept in a box. The arguments, I would for the majority of the time remain silent in fear, that he would do something crazy or hurt me. Over time, internally and physically I was dying inside. The enemy knew it, and it was only a matter of time that if I stayed I would have been dead. You know he knows our future as well. I was always told that I was a threat to the forces of darkness. From being overlooked to minister, to being mistreated from so called church people, I knew that what I carried was powerful. I began to see people for who they really were. In my new found singleness I had became. It took some time getting used to sleeping by myself. Thoughts of loneliness would creep in because, I was so used to having someone sleep next to me. God was doing something internally inside of me. I began to sleep with my worship music on at night. I began to pray daily without missing a beat. God and my relationship was on a whole different level. We had a friendship, a new found trust, and I realized that he really loves me and wanted what was best for me. It wasn't so bad being single. The divorce it shook me to the core. But the after affect was this peace that I had never experienced before. I understand now the scripture that says be anxious for nothing, but in everything in prayer and supplication, with thanksgiving, let your requests be made known unto God; and the peace of God, which surpasses all understanding, will guard your hearts and minds through Christ Jesus. I'd finally in my life experienced the peace of God. There was nothing no one could say or do that would change my mind into going back. This peace I was not willing to trade at all. I'd finally reach the epitome of finding what God had already had waiting for me. I had to walk through the door of realizing that I deserved better. I needed to be whole and set free in order to be effective for God's work. If that meant dropping the baggage off than so be it! I had to get where God was trying to get me to go and fast. I was not willing to forfeit another ten years of living in torment from a spirit that God allowed me to see. After I left, there were many prophecies that I did make the right choice. To piggyback on my dream, yes, I saw myself getting married to someone else and, my ex- husband was apologizing at the same time. God never showed me who that person was, but I knew that he was somewhere in my near future. It was easy for me to fall into the trap of self-criticism from the aftermath of dealing with a narcissist. It was one thing for me to take responsibility for the mistakes that I made-being hesitant to leave when I know that I needed to. I handed

out second, fourth, and fiftieth chances only to beat myself up with blame.
God reminded me I had to take care of myself as if taking care of a bad
illness. He is jealous for us and certainly does not want his children
abused. There is hope and there is an assurance that God can get
you out of any messes, especially the self-created ones.

Healing

Everything good that I believed about human beings were contradicted.
Every thought I had about loyalty, experience, and truthfulness was denied.
Every thought I had about marriage, love, and partnership was hammered
into silence. Every idea I had about the human connection was pretty
much trashed into his behaviors. You would think the emotional recovery
would be a walk in the park right? In many concluded relationships, after
the shouting has ended and called for our psychological immune system to
kick in, there comes a moment of calm and detachment when we are ready
to start over. Every promise that was made, every moment that was spent
together, everything you every believed about your relationship and
connection, had been burned to the ground. You aren't recovering from
love lost or even the failure of a marriage but from warfare.
 "Shell-shocked" is the word I would like to use as a survivor and it fits, as
does the military term "scorched earth", which I use to describe my ex
husband's legal maneuvers. What is wounding enough is, you will find
yourself revisiting what you thought was going on between the two of you,
and what really was. This is a biggie because what appeared to be about
two people was really about one. I studied what's called the misery of the

20/20 hindsight. These are the red flags that people always talk about – those signs that an intelligent person would never miss but you did. During the breakup they spring up like poppies, when everything you missed before or was hidden from view is suddenly plain sight.

I ended questioning my own judgement about everything, but then realized it was me that extended my hand to be led down that path. Once connecting the dots and seeing how I was made to relive the emotional moments again and again, by his control it didn't help me move on one bit. Nothing was what it seemed. It was easy to fall into self-criticism from the aftermath of a run in with him. I would think at times "only someone as dumb as me could have been taken by him", or there is something really wrong in me that I didn't see who he was". It's one thing to take responsibility for mistakes I made- being hesitant to leave when I know that I needed to, handing out second, third, and fiftieth chances-and another to beat myself up for connecting with him in the first place. In order to speed up my healing I began to surround myself with positive things. I tried very hard not to let my anger, resentment, and hurt destroy me. It literally ate away at my insides and almost turned me into a big ball of rage. Experiencing this depth of betrayal from someone I thought I could trust with my life cut away at my very soul. I made a conscious choice to get through it by sheer willpower. As for me, I was going to rise above the ashes and come out on the other end, stronger, and with my dignity. What I learned from this lesson was not to become embittered and wrongly apply that behavior to all individuals. If you hear yourself saying things like "all men are control freaks", or women will do anything to get their way, stop and remind yourself you are talking about one bad apple, not an orchard.

It's so easy to find yourself hosting your own pity party and submerging yourself in an ocean of self-criticism. First, instead of judging yourself, be kind and understanding. Rather than berating yourself for being stupid enough to get involved, be gentle and understand how you mistakenly thought the person was someone else. I found this experience as unique that anyone could find themselves in this situation. One other thing is forgiving yourself for not asking God if you should have got involved. A lot of times we make decisions not based on even asking God for his input. I am one of those who had to learn the hard way. If you don't know this, God desires to be a part of our everyday lives. He is not a magician, or we pick him up as needed, but he is always there. I found myself being so much in tune with worship, and just being wrapped up in his presence. My healing came through prayer, detox of my soul, mind, and body. I asked God to heal me of every emotional wound, heartbreak, and any other thing that I may have been missing. It's why he sent the Holy Spirit to help us. At times, we grieve him by making decisions that are not good ones. We have allowed people, or things to consume the place where he wants to dwell in our lives. A lot of times, those decisions are what allows havoc to wreak in our lives. It's a hard pill to swallow, but it's truth. I love you.

Counterfeit

I have always been told, and sure you have heard as well that the counterfeit always comes before the real thing. Oh yes, this isn't some kind old wise tells, and whoever said that is telling the truth. I can remember the dream that I had was so vivid. I saw myself getting remarried and facing my soon to be husband. God didn't allow me to see his face but, I saw myself sliding the wedding band on his finger. I was there in my wedding dress and he slid the ring on my finger as well. I noticed to the left that I saw my ex, and I could hear him apologizing that he was sorry. I then looked back to face my new husband and then I woke up. I remember telling my mother that I would never get married ever again. I also had told God that I was not as well. God does knows the desires of our hearts, and clearly says he knows the plans and purposes for our lives. How can I tell God what not to give me? I just figured that I would just focus on my non-profit and continue to work with the kids in Africa. This is where I told God he could have my whole life, and I would be totally dedicated to his work. I knew of a Pastor in Ghana that I had met through a mutual friend/social media. He already worked with the children in Ghana also. He had become quite fond of me, is what I took from it. Another evangelist as well as myself had decided that we would do a mission trip in February 2020 for a total of two weeks. This trip took a whole year to pre-plan from getting the visas, making sure we had passports, immunizations, and travel arrangements. When the time came to go, the other evangelist didn't have all her preparations taking care of and I had everything I needed. I was told that I would have a team waiting in Ghana to assist me for the two weeks that I would be there. The pastor that I knew organized the team there and I was told that I would have to speak, and work with the kids while there. While I was there in Ghana the Pastor had asked me to marry him. I took it as a confirmation of the dream I had of marrying someone else. I took it to God in prayer and didn't get any bad feelings about it, so I said yes. I thought to myself well why not? I would be spending a lot of time in in Africa so it made sense that my soon to be husband came from there. What I did not know was, in the process of wedding preparations Covid-19 would shut the borders down eight months. We were scheduled to marry on May 16, 2020. God has always had a sense of humor I would like to say. During this time of the world's uncertainty, God was still revealing. I took the time to stay in my word, push the non-profit but collecting shoes for the kids, and waiting. I began to see as well during this time what I attracted. It was the same spirit but accompanied by confusion, and lying. I had received a call as well on messenger from a woman questioning me about my relationship with the Pastor. I had missed the call, but the very next day I returned it. She didn't hesitate to send me the screenshots, messages, and call logs. Asking my then soon to be husband who she was and, what was that about, of course he lied. He immediately asked me to block her and that he needed peace in our relationship. Nothing form that point on would never ever be the same. I took a few days to pray and fast. During the waiting he had the audacity to be silent and play the victim. That was the classic sign of being with another narcissist. This time I was not going to be manipulated any longer. On top of everything he was asking this woman to send money as well. How many other victims were there out there? I knew then this was not his first encounter doing this. The money that we saved together because we opened a bank account in Ghana while I was there, he had nothing to show for it. I trusted that he was managing the account accordingly, but never the less he was using part of the money for expenses that were not his responsibility. When telling him that it was over, and that the wedding was off he thus decided to say that he hated me. A total of almost seven-thousand dollars we saved and you hated me? The majority of it was from what I saved. Upon realizing that I saw straight through him, the apology he offered was definitely to late. God gave me a dream that if I had married him, I would have given him a divorce. I took the pandemic as a way for God to stop me from making another terrible mistake. My discernment kicked up to a whole new level, and I was ready to kick down Hell's door now. Basic training was over, this meant war for the rest of my life. I was able to recognize the deceit and the counterfeit before saying I do. All I could say is God blocked it! He wouldn't let it be so.

Ashes Burned

God called me out of the ashes of oppression, and abuse. God gave me beauty where destruction and hopelessness had once tried to reside. I became something beautiful. The ashes of my life, God gave me a crown of beauty. For all of the years I mourned in that relationship he had given me the oil of joy. I emerged as new from something that had been destroyed in my life. Throughout the Bible and ancient practices, ashes have often been the symbol of deep repentance and grief. Sometimes it hurts. Sometimes it's tough. Sometimes it's dark. It leaves its mark, like the ashes of grief, in the deepest parts of our souls, where no one but God can really see. Yes, it's true, life is not always happy. It's not always easy. It deals harshly sometimes, it seems unfair, and we may wonder where God is, or why he didn't stop that difficult event or illness from happening. I have always compared my life to that of Job. He was the righteous man who loved and honored God. It crumbled around him, all he held dear. He knew without God, he was nothing. We find him in the beginning of the book of Job, "..He sat in the ashes." Job 2:8. What about Daniel? He and the people had suffered under captivity, he prayed to God on behalf of his people, that God would have mercy. He repented, and confessed his own

sin. "Then I turned my face to the Lord God, seeking him by prayer and

pleas for mercy with fasting and sackcloth and ashes." Daniel 9:3

Tamar was there. She had trusted and yet was betrayed. David's own

daughter had been taken advantage of, then was left on her own, alone,

with no hope for her future, to pick up the broken pieces of her shattered

life. "And Tamar put ashes on her head and tore the long robe that she

wore. And she laid her hand on her head and went away, crying aloud as

she went. 2 Samuel 13:19. Where is God in all this you may ask? Deep

grief, crime, illness, death of loved ones, shattered hope, and broken

dreams? His truth says this: He was, and is there in the midst of it all.

And though we may not always see it, or feel it, or even understand it, we

can know beyond a doubt, that He is now still with us. For he will never

leave us or forsake us, his love is greater than we can ever imagine,

though we live in a world where we face trouble many days. Jesus

reminds us in John 16:33, "In this world you will have trouble, but

take courage, for I have overcome the world." That's the very key to

the ashes that cover our days in this life. The deeper truth that

shines through every bit of our grief, pain, and sin. Christ came to set us

free in all areas. He came to redeem, and to bring hope. Christ came to

bring beauty from ashes. He never intends for us to stay stuck in our sin,

pain, or deep sorrow. He heals and restores. He calls us onward, and

reminds us that in him, we have great purpose and hope. There is beauty

and greatness behind every mark of darkness. The ashes will fall away,

they don't stay forever, but his greatness and glory shine forever through every broken place and flaw we've struggled through. Three days after Christ was buried…out of the dark, out of the dust, out of the tomb… He arose. Death had no hold on our Savior, and it has no hold on us, because the price He paid on our behalf. If I can leave you with this dear friends… God is greater that any enemy we face in this life. We overcome because He has overcome and our lives are hidden in Christ, May God Cover you with peace. May He bring healing in the face of hard news. May he bring deep abiding joy that makes no sense to the world. May he Bring comfort and care as He wraps you in his arms. The God of Miracles fights for you today, and he is mighty.

There is still beauty ahead…straight out of your ashes.

I love you
Debrecia

CPSIA information can be obtained
at www.ICGtesting.com
Printed in the USA
BVHW011118281220
596560BV00011B/598